D1302752

NATURE'S SUPERHEROES
SUPER ANTS

by Karen Latchana Kenney

pogo

Ideas for Parents and Teachers

Pogo Books let children practice reading informational text while introducing them to nonfiction features such as headings, labels, sidebars, maps, and diagrams, as well as a table of contents, glossary, and index.

Carefully leveled text with a strong photo match offers early fluent readers the support they need to succeed.

Before Reading

- "Walk" through the book and point out the various nonfiction features. Ask the student what purpose each feature serves.
- Look at the glossary together. Read and discuss the words.

Read the Book

- Have the child read the book independently.
- Invite him or her to list questions that arise from reading.

After Reading

- Discuss the child's questions. Talk about how he or she might find answers to those questions.
- Prompt the child to think more. Ask: What did you know about ants before you read this book? What more do you want to learn after reading it?

Pogo Books are published by Jump!
5357 Penn Avenue South
Minneapolis, MN 55419
www.jumplibrary.com

Library of Congress Cataloging-in-Publication Data

Names: Kenney, Karen Latchana, author.
Title: Super ants / by Karen Latchana Kenney.
Description: Minneapolis, MN: Jump!, Inc., [2018]
Series: Nature's superheroes | Audience: Ages 7–10.
Identifiers: LCCN 2017029248 (print)
LCCN 2017027721 (ebook)
ISBN 9781624967061 (ebook)
ISBN 9781620319246 (hardcover: alk. paper)
ISBN 9781620319666 (pbk.)
Subjects: LCSH: Ants—Juvenile literature.
Classification: LCC QL568.F7 (print)
LCC QL568.F7 K45 2017 (ebook) | DDC 595.79/6—dc23
LC record available at https://lccn.loc.gov/2017029248

Editor: Jenna Trnka
Book Designer: Michelle Sonnek
Photo Researcher: Michelle Sonnek

Photo Credits: NaturePL/SuperStock, cover, 1, 3; Redmond Durrell/Alamy, 4; Andrey Pavlov/Shutterstock, 5, 23; Doug Wechsler/Animals Animals, 6–7; Wlodarska/Shutterstock, 8; Donald Specker/Age Fotostock, 9; Michael McCoy/Getty, 10–11; Nature Picture Library/Alamy, 12–13; Mitsuhiko Imamori/Minden Pictures/SuperStock, 14–15; Minden Pictures/SuperStock, 16–17; Baby2M/Shutterstock, 18; Mr.Aukid Phumsirichat/Shutterstock, 19; Blickwinkel/Age Fotostock, 20–21.

Printed in the United States of America at Corporate Graphics in North Mankato, Minnesota.

TABLE OF CONTENTS

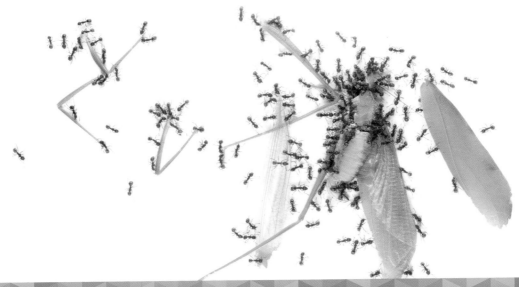

CHAPTER 1

SUPER INSECTS

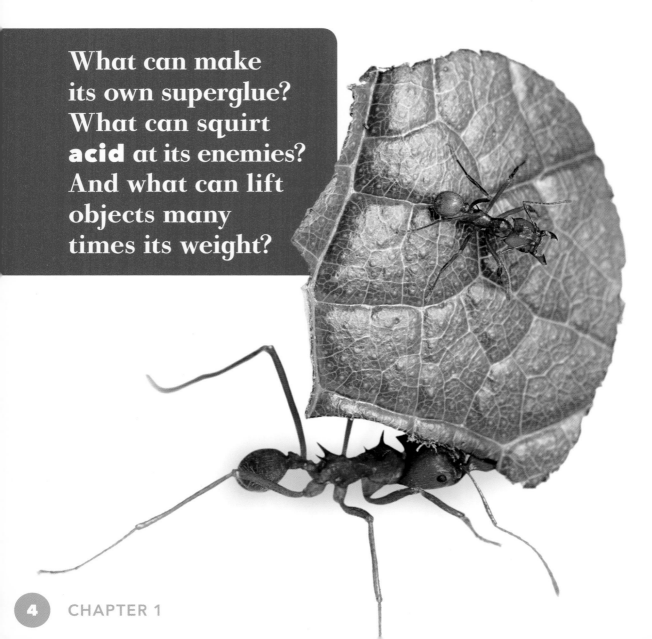

What can make its own superglue? What can squirt **acid** at its enemies? And what can lift objects many times its weight?

You might be surprised. It's tiny, but it has incredible powers. It's an ant!

Many kinds of ants live all around the world. These insects live in **colonies**. All ants in a colony are not the same. Large queens lay eggs. Soldiers protect the colony. Smaller workers build. They also care for **larvae** and find food. All have awesome powers.

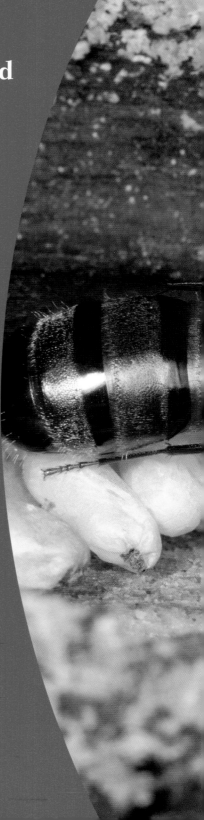

queen

larva

worker

CHAPTER 2

SUPERHERO POWERS

Ants are strong for their size. But mound ants are super strong. They build huge **mounds** on the forest floor. These nests house the colony.

Each mound ant can lift an object 5,000 times its own weight. That would be like a grown man lifting an airplane!

Ants build their nests in many ways. Weaver ants use leaves. And what else? Superglue. Larvae make sticky silk. Adult ants hold leaves together. Then an adult picks up a larva and squeezes it. The larva's silk glues the leaves together tight to make a nest.

Wood ants make their own stinky weapon. If a bird gets too close, they attack. The ants aim their **abdomens** in the air. Then they spray their **toxic** acid. The spray is smelly enough to scare the **predator** away.

DID YOU KNOW?

A Malaysian ant's body is filled with poison. Its body can explode when it is in danger. This kills the ant and its enemy.

In deserts, food can be hard to find. So some honey pot ants become living refrigerators. They hang from the ceiling of their nest. Workers feed them **nectar** from flowers. The nectar makes their abdomens blow up to the size of grapes! When food is low, the ants spit up some of their stored food for the colony.

A trap-jaw ant has the fastest bite in the world. Hairs cover the jaws. When they are touched, the jaws snap on **prey**. At high speeds, too! The jaws can close as fast as 145 miles (233 kilometers) per hour! That's about two times faster than cheetahs can run.

DID YOU KNOW?

A trap-jaw ant also uses its jaw to launch itself into the air. Some can jump higher than 1 foot (0.3 meters)!

prey

CHAPTER 3

HELPING THE COLONY

The many ants in a colony make it strong. Their powers make it stronger. Colonies can kill much larger creatures, such as scorpions and cockroaches.

The ants raid entire areas.
They take all the food they
can find. They use their
powers to keep the colony fed.

Ant powers help keep the colony safe. The ants use their powers to build and fix nests. The powers also make good defenses. They keep predators away. This way, the colony can continue to grow.